GLUTE
MEDITERR
COOKBOOK FOR
BEGINNER

"Simple and Delicious Gluten-Free Recipes for a Deliciously Healthy Mediterranean Diet"

By:

Ben Georg

Ben Georg

Copyright © Ben George
All right reserved

No part of book may be reproduced or stored in a retrieval system or transmitted in any form or by any means, electronic, mechanical, photocopying, recording or otherwise, without express written permission of the publisher

Table of content

Introduction 5

Basics of the Gluten-Free Mediterranean Diet 9

Shopping Tips for a Gluten-Free Mediterranean Diet .. 15

Preparing Meals with a Gluten-Free Mediterranean Diet
.... 19

Ingredients and pantry 25

Things to avoid with Ingredients and Pantry of Gluten-
Free Mediterranean Diet 29

Recipes: 37

Breakfast: 37

Launch 56

Dinner 74

Snack 89

Smoothies 104

Dessert: 117

Resources for Mediterranean diet 121

Appetizer and snacks 125

Vegetarian appetizer and snacks: 125

Sea food appetizer and snacks: 128

Meat appetizers and snacks 133

Soups and salad 137

Vegetarian soup and salad: 137

Seafood soups and salad 145

Meat soups and salad.. 166

Beverages 183

Vegetarian beverage: 183

Seafood beverage:.. 187

Meat beverage: 193

Conclusion 198

Introduction

Thomas was a 30 year old man who had been dealing with some nagging health issues. Despite visiting the doctor and trying different treatments, nothing seemed to work. He was feeling down and frustrated, and it seemed like he was running out of options.

One day, a friend of Thomas suggested that he try out the Mediterranean diet. He was a bit hesitant at first, but eventually decided to give it a try.

Thomas began by eliminating processed foods and replacing them with more whole, natural foods like fruits, vegetables, and grains. He also incorporated healthy fats like olive oil, nuts, and seeds into his diet. He also added more fish and lean proteins like chicken and legumes.

Within just a few weeks, Thomas noticed a big difference in his health. His energy levels increased, he was sleeping better, and his digestive issues had started to subside. After a few months of following the Mediterranean diet, Thomas was feeling better than ever and his health issues were completely gone.

Thomas was so pleased with the results that he decided to stick with the Mediterranean diet long-term. He now enjoys a healthy, balanced diet that gives him the energy and vitality he needs to live a happy and fulfilling life. He is so glad he gave the Mediterranean diet a chance, as it completely changed his life for the better.

The moral of the story is that a healthy diet can be a powerful tool in improving your health. Thomas was able to heal his health issues through the Mediterranean diet, and you too can benefit from the same approach.

So don't be afraid to give it a try! You never know what could be waiting on the other side.

Welcome to your Mediterranean Diet Cookbook for Beginners! This book is designed to help you learn how to cook delicious, healthy meals that are rooted in the Mediterranean diet. This type of diet has been proven to have multiple health benefits, including reducing the risk of heart disease and improving overall health.

In this cookbook, you'll find a variety of recipes that provide a taste of Mediterranean cuisine. From easy weeknight dinners to flavorful desserts, you'll find recipes that are simple to make and full of flavor. Plus, each recipe provides helpful tips on how to make the most of the ingredients and flavors found in Mediterranean cooking.

So, let's get started! With these recipes, you'll be able to bring the flavors of the Mediterranean to your kitchen. Bon appétit!

Basics of the Gluten-Free Mediterranean Diet

The Mediterranean diet is a popular way of eating that focuses on whole foods, plant-based foods, healthy fats, and moderate amounts of fish and poultry. The Mediterranean diet is free of gluten and other processed foods, and is considered one of the healthiest diets available.

This diet focuses on eating fruits, vegetables, legumes, nuts, whole grains, fish, and healthy fats such as olive oil. It also encourages moderate amounts of poultry, eggs, and dairy.

Red meat and processed foods are not part of the Mediterranean diet.

To get started on the Mediterranean diet, begin by incorporating more plant-based foods into your diet. Fruits, vegetables, legumes, nuts, and whole grains should form the foundation of the diet .Choose five to nine servings of fruits and vegetables per day as your goal. Healthy fats such as olive oil, nuts, and avocados should also be included in your diet.

Fish and poultry are also part of the Mediterranean diet. Aim for two to three servings of fish and poultry each week. Choose wild-caught, sustainable fish and poultry whenever possible.

The Mediterranean diet can be easily adapted to a gluten-free lifestyle. Be sure to read ingredient labels carefully and avoid processed foods that contain gluten. Make sure to choose gluten-free grains such as quinoa, buckwheat, and amaranth.

Overall, the Mediterranean diet is a healthy, balanced way of eating that is free of gluten. It focuses on whole, plant-based foods and encourages moderate amounts of fish and poultry. By following the Mediterranean diet, you can enjoy a variety of delicious and nutritious meals that are free of gluten.

The following are the main basics to consider as a beginner in eating Mediterranean diet

1. Focus on whole, plant-based foods such as fruits, vegetables, legumes, nuts, and whole grains.

2. Incorporate healthy fats such as olive oil, nuts, and avocados.

3. Include moderate amounts of fish and poultry. Choose wild-caught, sustainable fish and poultry whenever possible.

4. Avoid processed foods, especially those that contain gluten.

5. Read ingredient labels carefully to ensure that products are gluten-free.

6. Choose gluten-free grains such as quinoa, buckwheat, and amaranth.

7. Enjoy a variety of delicious and nutritious meals that are free of gluten.

Following these basics can help you reap the many health benefits of the Mediterranean diet, while still being able to enjoy gluten-free meals.

Ben Georg

Shopping Tips for a Gluten-Free Mediterranean Diet

1. Do your homework: Research the restaurants and stores that offer gluten-free options in your area. Many supermarkets, health food stores and specialty stores offer gluten-free versions of Mediterranean staples, such as olive oil, olives, fruits, and vegetables.

2. Read labels carefully: Take the time to read the ingredients in all packaged foods to make sure they are indeed gluten-free. Look for gluten-free labels and certifications on products.

3. Look for substitutes: If you're used to eating certain Mediterranean dishes, try to find gluten-free alternatives. Look for gluten-free pita chips, flatbreads, and other snacks.

4. Stock up on gluten-free ingredients: Stock your pantry with gluten-free staples such as olive oil, olives, tomatoes, and other ingredients used in Mediterranean cooking.

5. Grill it: Grilling is an excellent way to enjoy many Mediterranean dishes in a gluten-free way. Many grilled meats, fish, and vegetables are naturally gluten-free.

6. Make it yourself: Try making your own gluten-free Mediterranean dishes at home. You

can make delicious gluten-free versions of your favorite dishes with just a few simple ingredients.

7. Don't forget dessert: You don't have to give up dessert just because you're on a gluten-free diet. Look for gluten-free versions of Mediterranean desserts such as baklava and kataifi.

8. Enjoy the experience: Eating a gluten-free Mediterranean diet doesn't have to be a chore. Enjoy the flavors and the experience of discovering new foods and recipes.

9. Have fun: Eating a gluten-free Mediterranean diet can be fun and enjoyable. Experiment with

new recipes, explore the flavors of the region, and enjoy the food.

10. Be patient: Eating a gluten-free Mediterranean diet may take some getting used to, so be patient as you transition to a new way of eating.

Preparing Meals with a Gluten-Free Mediterranean Diet

Preparing meals with a gluten-free Mediterranean diet can be a challenge for some people, but with a little bit of creativity, it can be a delicious and healthy way to eat. The Mediterranean diet is based on the traditional foods of the countries bordering the Mediterranean Sea, such as Greece, Italy, and Spain. It typically includes plenty of vegetables, fruits, beans, nuts, seeds, whole grains, fish, and healthy fats such as olive oil.

The first step in preparing meals with a gluten-free Mediterranean diet is to plan ahead. Take the time to read labels and check for hidden sources of gluten. Common sources of hidden gluten include ingredients such as malt dextrin, modified food starch, natural flavors, and hydrolyzed vegetable protein. Also be sure to check for hidden sources of wheat, rye, and barley.

Once you have identified the gluten-free ingredients, you can start planning your menus. Focus on fresh and seasonal vegetables, fruits, whole grains, beans, nuts, seeds, fish, and healthy fats. Try to include a variety of flavors and textures in your dishes. For example, you could create a dish of roasted vegetables with feta cheese and olives, or a grilled salmon with roasted tomatoes and fresh herbs.

It's also important to pay attention to portion sizes. A good rule of thumb is to fill half of your plate with vegetables, one-quarter of your plate with a lean protein source such as fish or beans, and one-quarter of your plate with a whole grain.

Finally, don't be afraid to experiment with different flavors and ingredients. Try adding spices, herbs, and other flavorings to your dishes to make them more interesting. You'll find that following a gluten-free Mediterranean diet can be both delicious and nutritious.

With a little bit of planning and creativity, you can create delicious and nutritious gluten-free meals that are sure to please. So don't be intimidated by the gluten-free Mediterranean diet – with a little bit of know-how, you can prepare amazing meals that are both healthy and delicious.

The gluten-free Mediterranean diet is a diet that focuses on fresh, unprocessed foods such as fruits, vegetables, nuts, olive oil, and fish. It also eliminates wheat, barley, and rye, which are the main sources of gluten. This type of diet is a healthy way to lose weight, improve heart health, and reduce inflammation. When preparing meals with a gluten-free Mediterranean diet, focus on incorporating fresh ingredients that are rich in vitamins, minerals, and antioxidants. Start with a base of fresh vegetables, such as tomatoes, peppers, onions, and garlic. Then add healthy proteins such as fish, eggs, beans, and nuts. Finally, top off your meal with some fresh fruits and healthy fats, like olive oil and avocado. With its focus on fresh, unprocessed foods, this type of diet is a great way to enjoy a variety of delicious meals while also reaping the benefits of a healthy lifestyle.

Ben Georg

Ingredients and pantry

The Mediterranean diet is a well-known and widely accepted healthy eating plan that has been proven to reduce the risk of a variety of chronic diseases. It emphasizes the inclusion of whole grains, fresh fruits and vegetables, legumes, nuts, and healthy fats such as olive oil. Gluten-free Mediterranean diets are becoming more popular because they can be beneficial for those with celiac disease or gluten sensitivity.

The key ingredients in a gluten-free Mediterranean diet are whole grains, fruits and vegetables, legumes, nuts, and healthy fats such as olive oil. Whole grains, such as quinoa, teff, and rice, should be the basis of your meals. Fresh fruits and vegetables should be consumed in abundance, and legumes, such as lentils, chickpeas, and beans, can be added to salads, soups, and stews. Nuts and seeds, such as almonds, walnuts, and pumpkin seeds, can be added to salads and snacks, and healthy fats, such as olive oil, can be used for cooking and as dressings for salads.

In terms of pantry staples, a gluten-free Mediterranean diet should include gluten-free flours, such as almond flour, amaranth flour, and teff flour, as well as gluten-free pasta, quinoa, and rice. Other staples include canned beans, nuts, and seeds, and dried herbs and spices. A variety of gluten-free condiments, such as gluten-free soy sauce, vinegar, and tamari, can also be included.

By following a gluten-free Mediterranean diet, you can enjoy a wide variety of healthy and delicious meals that are rich in nutrients, vitamins, minerals, and healthy fats. With the right ingredients and pantry staples, you can easily create flavorful and nutritious meals that are sure to please.

Ben Georg

Things to avoid with Ingredients and Pantry of Gluten-Free Mediterranean Diet

1. Gluten-Free Breads and Pastas: Avoid any breads and pastas that contain wheat, barley, or rye. This includes some gluten-free breads and pastas that are made with wheat- or rye-based flours. Instead, opt for gluten-free breads and pastas made with rice, quinoa, corn, or other non-gluten containing grains.

2. Gluten-Containing Sauces and Dressings: Many sauces and dressings contain wheat, barley, or rye and should be avoided on a

gluten-free Mediterranean diet. Instead, make your own sauces and dressings with gluten-free ingredients like olive oil, garlic, herbs, and spices.

3. Gluten-Containing Dairy Products: Dairy products like cheese, yogurt, and milk can contain gluten. Be sure to read labels and check for gluten-containing ingredients before consuming. If in doubt, opt for gluten-free dairy products like lactose-free milk, or almond, coconut, or soy milk.

4. Gluten-Containing Grains: Grains such as wheat, barley, and rye should be avoided on a gluten-free Mediterranean diet. Instead, opt for gluten-free grains like quinoa, buckwheat, amaranth, and millet.

5. Gluten-Containing Processed Foods and Sweets: Processed foods, sweets, and snacks often contain gluten. Be sure to read labels carefully to ensure that these items are gluten-free before consuming.

6. Gluten-Containing Beverages: Some alcoholic beverages, like beer and some wines, contain gluten. Be sure to check labels before consuming. Instead, opt for gluten-free beverages like wine, cider, and spirits.

7. Gluten-Containing Flours: Gluten-containing flours, such as wheat, barley, and rye should be avoided on a gluten-free Mediterranean diet. Instead, opt for gluten-free flours like almond, coconut, buckwheat, and quinoa.

8. Gluten-Containing Oils and Fats: Oils and fats can contain gluten, so be sure to check labels and opt for gluten-free alternatives like olive oil and coconut oil.

9. Gluten-Containing Spices: Some spices contain gluten, so be sure to read labels carefully before using. Instead, opt for gluten-free spices like garlic, cumin, turmeric, and paprika.

10. Gluten-Containing Additives and Preservatives: Many additives and preservatives can contain gluten, so be sure to read labels and opt for gluten-free alternatives.

Ben Georg

Tools and Equipment

The Gluten-Free Mediterranean Diet is a way of eating that is based on the traditional dietary patterns of countries around the Mediterranean Sea. This style of eating emphasizes vegetables, fruits, whole grains, legumes, nuts, and healthy fats. It also avoids processed foods, refined sugars, and unhealthy fats. Those following a gluten-free Mediterranean diet should be sure to check labels carefully, as some processed foods may contain gluten.

Tools and equipment that are important for following a gluten-free Mediterranean diet include a good quality blender or food processor, a good set of kitchen knives, a cutting board, and a variety of cooking pots, pans, and baking dishes. A good set of measuring cups and spoons is also essential for measuring ingredients accurately. Kitchen scales and a timer are also helpful for measuring and tracking food portions, and a food thermometer can help ensure that food is cooked to the proper temperature for optimal safety.

For those who have difficulty preparing their own meals, there are a number of prepared gluten-free options available at the grocery store. These options can provide a convenient and tasty way to get the nutrients needed for a healthy diet. Additionally, there are a number of cookbooks and websites dedicated to gluten-free Mediterranean recipes, which can make meal planning easier.

Overall, the Gluten-Free Mediterranean Diet is a healthy and delicious way to eat. With the right tools and equipment, and some careful label reading, those following the diet can enjoy a variety of delicious and nutritious meals.

Recipes:

Breakfast:

1. Mediterranean Frittata:

Introduction: Start your day with this Mediterranean-inspired dish of frittata loaded with spinach, tomatoes, bell peppers, feta cheese and olives.

Ingredients:

• 6 large eggs

• 2 tablespoons olive oil

• 1 cup chopped spinach

• 1/2 cup diced tomatoes

• 1/2 cup diced bell peppers

• 1/4 cup crumbled feta cheese

• 2 tablespoons chopped black olives

• Salt and pepper to taste

Preparation:

1. Preheat the oven to 350 degrees.

2. In a medium bowl, whisk together the eggs, olive oil, spinach, tomatoes, bell peppers, feta cheese, olives, salt and pepper.

3. Pour the egg mixture into a greased 9-inch baking dish and bake for 25 minutes or until the center is set.

Prep time: 10 minutes

2. Mediterranean Veggie Omelet:

Introduction: This savory and flavorful omelet is filled with plenty of veggies and is a great way to start your day.

Ingredients:

• 3 large eggs

• 2 tablespoons olive oil

• 1/2 cup diced tomatoes

• 1/2 cup diced bell peppers

• 1/4 cup crumbled feta cheese

• 2 tablespoons chopped black olives

• Salt and pepper to taste

Preparation:

1. Heat the olive oil in a medium skillet over medium heat.

2. In a medium bowl, whisk together the eggs, tomatoes, bell peppers, feta cheese, olives, salt and pepper.

3. Pour the egg mixture into the skillet and cook for 3-4 minutes, until the edges are set.

4. Flip the omelet and cook for an additional 1-2 minutes.

Prep time: 10 minutes

3. Mediterranean Egg Toast:

Introduction: Start your day with a delicious and nutritious breakfast of Mediterranean-style egg toast, filled with feta cheese, spinach, and olives.

Ingredients:

- 2 slices gluten-free bread

- 2 tablespoons olive oil

- 2 large eggs

- 1/2 cup chopped spinach

- 1/4 cup crumbled feta cheese

- 2 tablespoons chopped black olives

- Salt and pepper to taste

Preparation:

1. Heat a medium skillet over medium heat and add 1 tablespoon of olive oil.

2. Crack the eggs into the skillet and cook for 2-3 minutes, until the whites are set.

3. Toast the bread and spread the remaining olive oil on each slice.

4. Divide the spinach, feta cheese and olives among the slices of toast.

5. Top with the cooked eggs and season with salt and pepper.

Prep time: 10 minutes

4. Mediterranean Yogurt Bowl:

Introduction: Start your day with this delicious and nutritious Mediterranean-style yogurt bowl, filled with fresh fruit, nuts, and honey.

Ingredients:

• 1 cup plain Greek yogurt

• 1/2 cup fresh fruit, such as blueberries, strawberries, and/or banana slices

• 2 tablespoons chopped walnuts

• 2 tablespoons honey

• 1 tablespoon toasted coconut flakes

• 1 tablespoon chia seeds

Preparation:

1. In a medium bowl, combine the yogurt, fruit, walnuts, honey, coconut flakes, and chia seeds.

2. Stir to combine and transfer to a serving bowl.

Prep time: 5 minutes

5. Mediterranean Avocado Toast:

Introduction: Start your day with this healthy and flavorful Mediterranean-style avocado toast, topped with feta cheese, tomatoes, and olives.

Ingredients:

• 2 slices gluten-free bread

• 1 avocado, mashed

• 2 tablespoons olive oil

• 1/4 cup diced tomatoes

• 1/4 cup crumbled feta cheese

• 2 tablespoons chopped black olives

• Salt and pepper to taste

Preparation:

1. Toast the bread and spread the mashed avocado on each slice.

2. Top with the tomatoes, feta cheese, and olives, and season with salt and pepper.

3. Drizzle with olive oil and serve.

Prep time: 5 minutes

6. Mediterranean Egg Muffins:

Introduction: Enjoy these savory and flavorful Mediterranean-style egg muffins, filled with spinach, tomatoes, bell peppers, feta cheese, and olives.

Ingredients:

- 6 large eggs

- 2 tablespoons olive oil

- 1 cup chopped spinach

- 1/2 cup diced tomatoes

- 1/2 cup diced bell peppers

- 1/4 cup crumbled feta cheese

- 2 tablespoons chopped black olives

- Salt and pepper to taste

Preparation:

1. Preheat the oven to 350 degrees.

2. Grease a 12-cup muffin tin with olive oil.

3. In a medium bowl, whisk together the eggs, olive oil, spinach, tomatoes, bell peppers, feta cheese, olives, salt and pepper.

4. Divide the egg mixture evenly among the muffin cups and bake for 20 minutes, or until the centers are set.

Prep time: 10 minutes

7. Mediterranean Vegetable Hash:

Introduction: Enjoy this delicious and nutritious dish of Mediterranean-style vegetable hash, filled with sweet potatoes, bell peppers, onions, and olives.

Ingredients:

• 2 tablespoons olive oil

• 2 cups diced sweet potatoes

• 1 cup diced bell peppers

• 1 cup diced onions

• 2 tablespoons chopped black olives

• Salt and pepper to taste

Preparation:

1. Heat the olive oil in a large skillet over medium heat.

2. Add the sweet potatoes, bell peppers, onions, and olives to the skillet and season with salt and pepper.

3. Cook, stirring occasionally, for 10-12 minutes, or until the vegetables are tender.

Prep time: 10 minutes

8. Mediterranean Breakfast Burrito:

Introduction: Enjoy this delicious and filling Mediterranean-style breakfast burrito, filled with scrambled eggs, olives, feta cheese, and spinach.

Ingredients:

• 1 large gluten-free tortilla

• 3 large eggs

• 2 tablespoons olive oil

- 1/4 cup chopped spinach

- 1/4 cup crumbled feta cheese

- 2 tablespoons chopped black olives

- Salt and pepper to taste

Preparation:

1. In a medium bowl, whisk together the eggs, olive oil, spinach, feta cheese, olives, salt and pepper.

2. Heat a medium skillet over medium heat and add the egg mixture.

3. Cook for 3-4 minutes, until the eggs are set.

Prep time: 10 minutes

4. Place the egg mixture on the tortilla and top with additional feta cheese, olives, and spinach.

5. Roll up the burrito and enjoy.

9. Mediterranean Fruit Bowl:

Introduction: Enjoy this healthy and delicious Mediterranean-style fruit bowl, filled with fresh fruit, nuts, and honey.

Ingredients:

• 1 cup diced fresh fruit, such as strawberries, blueberries, and/or banana slices

• 2 tablespoons chopped walnuts

• 2 tablespoons honey

• 1 tablespoon toasted coconut flakes

• 1 tablespoon chia seeds

Preparation:

1. In a medium bowl, combine the fruit, walnuts, honey, coconut flakes, and chia seeds.

2. Stir to combine and transfer to a serving bowl.

Prep time: 5 minutes

10. Mediterranean Smoothie Bowl:

Introduction: Enjoy this delicious and nutritious breakfast smoothie bowl, filled with yogurt, banana, walnuts, and honey.

Ingredients:

- 1 cup plain Greek yogurt

- 1 banana, sliced

- 2 tablespoons chopped walnuts

- 2 tablespoons honey

- 1 tablespoon toasted coconut flakes

- 1 tablespoon chia seeds

Preparation:

1. In a blender, combine the yogurt, banana, walnuts, honey, coconut flakes, and chia seeds.

2. Blend until smooth and transfer to a serving bowl.

Prep time: 5 minutes

Ben Georg

Ben Georg

Launch

1. Greek-Style Grilled Vegetables (Prep time: 10 minutes): This Mediterranean-inspired dish is a delicious way to get your daily dose of vegetables. It is easy to make and gluten-free. Simply cut up your favorite vegetables, such as bell peppers, onions, zucchini, and mushrooms, and toss them with olive oil, garlic, oregano, and salt and pepper. Grill the vegetables over medium-high heat until they are tender. Serve with a squeeze of fresh lemon juice.

Ingredients:

• 2 bell peppers, sliced

• 1 onion, sliced

• 2 zucchinis, sliced

• 8 ounces mushrooms, sliced

- 3 tablespoons olive oil

- 2 cloves garlic, minced

- 2 teaspoons dried oregano

- Salt and pepper to taste

- Lemon juice, to serve

Preparation:

1. Preheat the grill to medium-high heat.

2. In a large bowl, combine the bell peppers, onion, zucchini, mushrooms, olive oil, garlic, oregano, salt, and pepper.

3. Grill the vegetables in batches until they are tender.

4. Serve with a squeeze of fresh lemon juice.

2. Mediterranean Baked Salmon (Prep time: 15 minutes): This easy and delicious dish is perfect for a weeknight meal. It is packed with flavor and nutrition, and it is gluten-free. Simply bake the salmon with a mixture of olive oil, garlic, oregano, lemon juice, and capers. Serve with a side of roasted vegetables for a complete meal.

Ingredients:

• 4 (4-ounce) salmon fillets

• 3 tablespoons olive oil

• 2 cloves garlic, minced

• 2 teaspoons dried oregano

• 2 tablespoons lemon juice

• 2 tablespoons capers

• Salt and pepper to taste

Preparation:

1. Preheat the oven to 375°F.

2. Place the salmon fillets on a baking sheet.

3. In a small bowl, combine the olive oil, garlic, oregano, lemon juice, capers, salt, and pepper.

4. Pour the mixture over the salmon fillets.

5. Bake for 15 minutes, or until the salmon is cooked through.

3. Quinoa Salad with Feta and Olives (Prep time: 10 minutes): This salad is a great way to get your daily dose of protein and fiber. It is also a gluten-free dish. Simply cook the quinoa and combine it with feta cheese, olives, red

onion, and a light vinaigrette. Serve with a side of grilled chicken or fish for a complete meal.

Ingredients:

- 1 cup quinoa, cooked

- 1/2 cup feta cheese, crumbled

- 1/4 cup olives, chopped

- 1/4 cup red onion, diced

- 2 tablespoons olive oil

- 1 tablespoon red wine vinegar

- 1 teaspoon Dijon mustard

- Salt and pepper to taste

Preparation:

1. In a large bowl, combine the cooked quinoa, feta cheese, olives, and red onion.

2. In a small bowl, whisk together the olive oil, red wine vinegar, Dijon mustard, salt, and pepper.

3. Pour the dressing over the quinoa mixture and toss to combine.

4. Serve with grilled chicken or fish.

4. Greek Yogurt with Honey and Berries (Prep time: 5 minutes): This quick and easy snack is a delicious way to get your daily dose of calcium and protein. It is also gluten-free. Simply combine plain Greek yogurt with honey and your favorite berries. Enjoy as a snack or a light dessert.

Ingredients:

• 2 cups plain Greek yogurt

• 2 tablespoons honey

• 1 cup berries, such as raspberries, blueberries, or blackberries

Preparation:

1. In a medium bowl, combine the Greek yogurt and honey.

2. Stir in the berries.

3. Serve immediately.

5. Mediterranean Quiche (Prep time: 15 minutes): This tasty quiche is a delicious way to get your daily dose of vegetables and protein. It

is also gluten-free. Simply combine eggs, vegetables, feta cheese, and a light cream sauce. Bake until the quiche is golden brown and the filling is set.

Ingredients:

- 6 eggs

- 1/2 cup bell peppers, chopped

- 1/2 cup mushrooms, chopped

- 1/2 cup feta cheese, crumbled

- 1/2 cup cream

- 1/2 teaspoon dried oregano

- Salt and pepper to taste

Preparation:

1. Preheat the oven to 375°F.

2. In a large bowl, whisk together the eggs, bell peppers, mushrooms, feta cheese, cream, oregano, salt, and pepper.

3. Pour the mixture into a 9-inch pie dish.

4. Bake for 15 minutes, or until the quiche is golden brown and the filling is set.

6. Baked Falafel (Prep time: 10 minutes): This tasty and easy-to-make dish is a great way to get your daily dose of protein and fiber. It is also gluten-free. Simply mix together chickpeas, garlic, and herbs, and shape the mixture into patties. Bake until golden brown. Serve with tahini sauce and a side of vegetables.

Ingredients:

- 2 (15-ounce) cans chickpeas, drained and rinsed

- 2 cloves garlic, minced

- 1/4 cup fresh parsley, chopped

- 1/4 cup fresh cilantro, chopped

- 2 tablespoons olive oil

- 2 teaspoons ground cumin

- 1 teaspoon baking powder

- Salt and pepper to taste

Preparation:

1. Preheat the oven to 375°F.

2. In a food processor, combine the chickpeas, garlic, parsley, cilantro, olive oil, cumin, baking

powder, salt, and pepper. Process until the mixture is well combined.

3. Shape the mixture into 2-inch patties.

4. Place the patties on a baking sheet lined with parchment paper.

5. Bake for 10 minutes, or until the falafel are golden brown.

6. Serve with tahini sauce and a side of vegetables.

7. Roasted Eggplant Dip (Prep time: 10 minutes): This flavorful dip is a great way to get your daily dose of vegetables. It is also gluten-free. Simply roast the eggplant with garlic and herbs, and combine it with tahini, lemon juice, and olive oil. Serve with your favorite vegetables or pita chips.

Ingredients:

- 1 large eggplant, chopped

- 2 cloves garlic, minced

- 1 tablespoon olive oil

- 2 teaspoons dried oregano

- 1/4 cup tahini

- 2 tablespoons lemon juice

- Salt and pepper to taste

Preparation:

1. Preheat the oven to 375°F.

2. In a large bowl, combine the eggplant, garlic, olive oil, oregano, salt, and pepper.

3. Place the eggplant mixture on a baking sheet lined with parchment paper.

4. Roast for 10 minutes, or until the eggplant is tender.

5. In a food processor, combine the roasted eggplant, tahini, and lemon juice. Process until the mixture is smooth.

6. Serve with your favorite vegetables or pita chips.

8. Hummus and Veggie Wrap (Prep time: 10 minutes): This tasty wrap is a great way to get your daily dose of protein and fiber. It is also gluten-free. Simply spread hummus on a wrap and top it with your favorite vegetables. Roll it up and enjoy.

Ingredients:

- 1 whole-wheat wrap

- 1/4 cup hummus

- 1/2 cup bell peppers, sliced

- 1/2 cup cucumber, sliced

- 1/4 cup red onion, diced

- 2 tablespoons fresh parsley, chopped

- 2 tablespoons olive oil

- Salt and pepper to taste

Preparation:

1. Spread the hummus on the wrap.

2. Top with the bell peppers, cucumber, red onion, and parsley.

3. Drizzle with the olive oil and sprinkle with salt and pepper.

4. Roll up the wrap and enjoy.

9. Mediterranean Tofu Salad (Prep time: 10 minutes): This tasty salad is a great way to get your daily dose of protein and fiber. It is also gluten-free. Simply combine cooked quinoa, tofu, olives, and a light vinaigrette. Serve with a side of grilled chicken or fish for a complete meal.

Ingredients:

• 1 cup quinoa, cooked

• 8 ounces firm tofu, diced

• 1/2 cup olives, chopped

- 2 tablespoons olive oil

- 1 tablespoon red wine vinegar

- 1 teaspoon Dijon mustard

- Salt and pepper to taste

Preparation:

1. In a large bowl, combine the cooked quinoa, tofu, and olives.

2. In a small bowl, whisk together the olive oil, red wine vinegar, Dijon mustard, salt, and pepper.

3. Pour the dressing over the quinoa mixture and toss to combine.

4. Serve with grilled chicken or fish.

10. Grilled Seafood Skewers (Prep time: 10 minutes): This easy and delicious dish is perfect for a weeknight meal. It is packed with protein and flavor, and it is gluten-free. Simply marinate your favorite seafood in a mixture of olive oil, garlic, oregano, and lemon juice. Grill the skewers until the seafood is cooked through. Serve with a side of roasted vegetables for a complete meal.

Ingredients:

• 8 ounces shrimp, peeled and deveined

• 8 ounces scallops

• 8 ounces squid, cleaned and cut into 1-inch pieces

• 3 tablespoons olive oil

• 2 cloves garlic, minced

• 2 teaspoons dried oregano

• 2 tablespoons lemon juice

• Salt and pepper to taste

Preparation:

1. Preheat the grill to medium-high heat.

2. In a medium bowl, combine the shrimp, scallops, squid, olive oil, garlic, oregano, lemon juice, salt, and pepper.

3. Thread the seafood onto skewers.

4. Grill the skewers for 5 minutes per side, or until the seafood is cooked through.

5. Serve with a side of roasted vegetables.

Dinner

1. Mediterranean Stuffed Peppers:

Introduction: These Mediterranean Stuffed Peppers are full of flavor and the perfect gluten-free dinner!

Ingredients: 4 bell peppers, 1 can chickpeas (drained and rinsed), 1/2 cup diced red onion, 1/2 cup diced red pepper, 1/2 cup diced zucchini, 2 garlic cloves (minced), 1/2 teaspoon ground cumin, 1/2 teaspoon smoked paprika, 1/4 cup crumbled feta cheese, 1/4 cup chopped fresh parsley, 1/4 cup pine nuts, 2 tablespoons extra-virgin olive oil, Salt, and black pepper.

Preparation: Preheat oven to 400°F. Cut the peppers in half lengthwise and remove the seeds and veins. Place the peppers in a baking dish.

In a medium bowl, combine the chickpeas, onion, red pepper, zucchini, garlic, cumin, smoked paprika, feta cheese, parsley, pine nuts, olive oil, salt, and pepper. Mix until well combined.

Fill the pepper halves with the mixture and bake for 25 minutes. Serve warm.

Prep Time: 10 minutes.

2. Mediterranean Salmon with Roasted Potatoes:

Introduction: This Mediterranean Salmon with Roasted Potatoes is a delicious and healthy gluten-free dinner.

Ingredients: 2 tablespoons extra-virgin olive oil, divided, 2 cloves garlic (minced), 2 tablespoons freshly chopped oregano, 2 tablespoons freshly chopped parsley, Juice of 1/2 lemon, 2 large potatoes (diced), 2 salmon fillets, Salt, and black pepper.

Preparation: Preheat oven to 400°F. In a small bowl, combine 1 tablespoon of olive oil, garlic, oregano, parsley, and lemon juice. Mix until well combined and set aside.

In a baking dish, add the potatoes and season with salt and pepper. Drizzle with 1 tablespoon of olive oil and mix until the potatoes are evenly coated.

Add the salmon fillets to the baking dish and brush the top of each fillet with the garlic-herb mixture. Bake for 20 minutes or until the salmon is cooked through. Serve warm.

Prep Time: 10 minutes.

3. Mediterranean Quinoa Salad:

Introduction: This Mediterranean Quinoa Salad is a light and delicious gluten-free dinner.

Ingredients: 1 cup quinoa (rinsed and drained), 2 cups vegetable broth, 2 tablespoons extra-virgin olive oil, 1/2 cup diced red onion, 1/2 cup diced red pepper, 1/2 cup diced cucumber, 1/2 cup diced tomatoes, 2 tablespoons freshly chopped parsley, 1/4 cup crumbled feta cheese, Juice of 1/2 lemon, Salt, and black pepper.

Preparation: In a medium saucepan, add the quinoa and vegetable broth. Bring to a boil over medium-high heat. Reduce heat to low and simmer for 15 minutes or until the quinoa is cooked through.

In a large bowl, combine the quinoa, olive oil, onion, red pepper, cucumber, tomatoes, parsley, feta cheese, lemon juice, salt, and pepper. Mix until well combined.

Serve warm or chilled.

Prep Time: 10 minutes.

4. Mediterranean Zucchini Noodles with Shrimp:

Introduction: These Mediterranean Zucchini Noodles with Shrimp are a light and healthy gluten-free dinner.

Ingredients: 2 tablespoons extra-virgin olive oil, 4 cloves garlic (minced), 1/2 teaspoon red pepper flakes, 1/2 teaspoon dried oregano, 1/2 teaspoon dried basil, 1/2 teaspoon dried thyme, 2 zucchini (spiralized), 1 cup cherry tomatoes (halved), 1/2 cup white wine, 1 pound shrimp (peeled and deveined), 1/4 cup freshly chopped parsley, Salt, and black pepper.

Preparation: Heat the olive oil in a large skillet over medium-high heat. Add the garlic and red pepper flakes and cook for 1 minute.

Add the oregano, basil, and thyme and cook for another minute.

Add the zucchini noodles and cherry tomatoes and cook for 2 minutes.

Add the white wine, shrimp, parsley, salt, and pepper. Cook for 5 minutes or until the shrimp are cooked through.

Serve warm.

Prep Time: 10 minutes.

5. Mediterranean Cauliflower Rice Bowl:

Introduction: This Mediterranean Cauliflower Rice Bowl is a healthy and flavorful gluten-free dinner.

Ingredients: 2 tablespoons extra-virgin olive oil, 1 head cauliflower (grated), 1/2 cup diced red onion, 2 cloves garlic (minced), 1/2 teaspoon ground cumin, 1/2 teaspoon smoked paprika, 1/2 cup cooked chickpeas, 1/2 cup diced tomatoes, 1/2 cup cooked quinoa, 1/4 cup crumbled feta cheese, 1/4 cup freshly chopped parsley, Salt, and black pepper.

Preparation: Heat the olive oil in a large skillet over medium-high heat. Add the cauliflower, onion, garlic, cumin, and smoked paprika. Cook for 5 minutes or until the cauliflower is tender.

Add the chickpeas, tomatoes, quinoa, feta cheese, parsley, salt, and pepper. Cook for another 5 minutes or until the quinoa is heated through.

Serve warm.

Prep Time: 10 minutes.

6. Mediterranean Vegetable Soup:

Introduction: This Mediterranean Vegetable Soup is a hearty and comforting gluten-free dinner.

Ingredients: 2 tablespoons extra-virgin olive oil, 1 onion (diced), 2 carrots (diced), 2 celery stalks (diced), 2 cloves garlic (minced), 1 teaspoon dried oregano, 1 teaspoon dried basil, 1 teaspoon dried thyme, 4 cups vegetable broth, 1 can diced tomatoes (undrained), 1 can chickpeas (drained and rinsed), 2 cups kale (chopped), Salt, and black pepper.

Preparation: Heat the olive oil in a large pot over medium-high heat. Add the onion, carrots, celery, garlic, oregano, basil, and thyme. Cook for 5 minutes or until the vegetables are tender.

Add the vegetable broth, tomatoes, chickpeas, and kale. Bring to a boil and reduce heat to low. Simmer for 20 minutes or until the vegetables are tender.

Season with salt and pepper to taste. Serve warm.

Prep Time: 10 minutes.

7. Mediterranean Tuna Salad:

Introduction: This Mediterranean Tuna Salad is a light and healthy gluten-free dinner.

Ingredients: 2 cans tuna (drained), 1/2 cup diced cucumber, 1/2 cup diced tomatoes, 1/2 cup diced red onion, 1/4 cup crumbled feta cheese, 2 tablespoons freshly chopped parsley, 2 tablespoons freshly chopped oregano, Juice of

1/2 lemon, 2 tablespoons extra-virgin olive oil, Salt, and black pepper.

Preparation: In a large bowl, combine the tuna, cucumber, tomatoes, onion, feta cheese, parsley, oregano, lemon juice, olive oil, salt, and pepper. Mix until well combined.

Serve chilled or at room temperature.

Prep Time: 10 minutes.

8. Mediterranean Eggplant:

Introduction: This Mediterranean Eggplant is a flavorful and healthy gluten-free dinner.

Ingredients: 2 tablespoons extra-virgin olive oil, 2 cloves garlic (minced), 1 teaspoon dried oregano, 1 teaspoon dried basil, 1 teaspoon dried thyme, 1 eggplant (diced), 1 cup diced tomatoes, 1/2 cup crumbled feta cheese, Juice of 1/2 lemon, Salt, and black pepper.

Preparation: Heat the olive oil in a large skillet over medium-high heat. Add the garlic, oregano, basil, and thyme and cook for 1 minute.

Add the eggplant and cook for 5 minutes or until the eggplant is tender.

Add the tomatoes, feta cheese, lemon juice, salt, and pepper. Cook for another 5 minutes or until the tomatoes are softened.

Serve warm.

Prep Time: 10 minutes.

9. Mediterranean Lentil Salad:

Introduction: This Mediterranean Lentil Salad is a light and delicious gluten-free dinner.

Ingredients: 2 cups cooked green lentils, 1/2 cup diced red onion, 1/2 cup diced red pepper, 1/2 cup diced cucumber, 1/4 cup crumbled feta cheese, 2 tablespoons freshly chopped parsley, 2 tablespoons freshly chopped oregano, 2 tablespoons freshly chopped mint, Juice of 1/2 lemon, 2 tablespoons extra-virgin olive oil, Salt, and black pepper.

Preparation: In a large bowl, combine the lentils, onion, red pepper, cucumber, feta cheese, parsley, oregano, mint, lemon juice, olive oil, salt, and pepper. Mix until well combined.

Serve chilled or at room temperature.

Prep Time: 10 minutes.

10. Mediterranean Roasted Vegetables:

Introduction: These Mediterranean Roasted Vegetables are a delicious and healthy gluten-free dinner.

Ingredients: 2 tablespoons extra-virgin olive oil, 2 cloves garlic (minced), 1/2 teaspoon dried oregano, 1/2 teaspoon dried basil, 1/2 teaspoon dried thyme, 2 zucchini (sliced), 2 yellow squash (sliced), 2 red bell peppers (diced), 2 carrots (diced), 2 tablespoons freshly chopped parsley, Salt, and black pepper.

Preparation: Preheat oven to 400°F. In a large bowl, combine the olive oil, garlic, oregano, basil, and thyme. Mix until well combined.

Add the zucchini, yellow squash, bell peppers, carrots, and parsley. Mix until the vegetables are evenly coated.

Transfer the vegetables to a baking sheet and season with salt and pepper.

Bake for 25 minutes or until the vegetables are tender.

Serve warm.

Prep Time: 10 minutes.

Ben Georg

Snack

1. Hummus with Pita Chips: Hummus is a classic Mediterranean snack, and it's easy to make. Just combine cooked chickpeas, tahini, garlic, lemon juice, and olive oil in a food processor. Serve with whole wheat pita chips for a delicious and healthy snack.

Ingredients:

-1 can chickpeas, rinsed and drained

-1/4 cup tahini

-1 garlic clove, minced

-2 tablespoons lemon juice

-2 tablespoons olive oil

-Whole wheat pita chips

Preparation Method:

-Combine chickpeas, tahini, garlic, lemon juice, and olive oil in a food processor. Blend until smooth.

-Spread hummus onto a plate and serve with pita chips.

Prep Time: 10 minutes

2. Greek Yogurt with Fruit: Greek yogurt is a staple of the Mediterranean diet. Top plain Greek yogurt with your favorite fresh fruit for a healthy and satisfying snack.

Ingredients:

-1 cup plain Greek yogurt

-1 cup fresh fruit, diced

Preparation Method:

-Spoon yogurt into a bowl.

-Top with diced fruit.

Prep Time: 5 minutes

3. Tomato and Mozzarella Skewers: This snack combines two classic Mediterranean flavors – tomatoes and mozzarella. Skewer pieces of tomato and mozzarella, then drizzle with olive oil and fresh basil.

Ingredients:

-1 pint cherry tomatoes

-1 ball fresh mozzarella, cubed

-2 tablespoons olive oil

-2 tablespoons fresh basil, chopped

Preparation Method:

-Thread tomatoes and mozzarella onto skewers.

-Drizzle with olive oil and sprinkle with fresh basil.

Prep Time: 10 minutes

4. Mediterranean Veggie Platter: For a light snack, serve a veggie platter with hummus.

Arrange cucumbers, carrots, bell peppers, and olives on a plate. Serve with hummus for dipping.

Ingredients:

-1 cucumber, sliced

-2 carrots, sliced

-1 bell pepper, sliced

-1/2 cup olives

-1/2 cup hummus

Preparation Method:

-Arrange cucumbers, carrots, bell peppers, and olives on a plate.

-Serve with hummus for dipping.

Prep Time: 10 minutes

5. Baked Eggplant Chips: Eggplant is a staple in Mediterranean cooking. For a healthy snack, slice eggplant into thin slices and bake until crispy. Serve with a side of Greek yogurt dip.

Ingredients:

-1 large eggplant, sliced

-1 tablespoon olive oil

-1/2 teaspoon sea salt

-1/2 cup plain Greek yogurt

-1 garlic clove, minced

-1 tablespoon lemon juice

Preparation Method:

-Preheat oven to 400°F.

-Arrange eggplant slices on a baking sheet and brush with olive oil. Sprinkle with sea salt.

-Bake for 20 minutes, flipping halfway through.

-In a small bowl, combine Greek yogurt, garlic, and lemon juice.

-Serve eggplant chips with Greek yogurt dip.

Prep Time: 30 minutes

6. Mediterranean Quesadilla: For a heartier snack, try a Mediterranean-inspired quesadilla.

Spread hummus on a whole wheat tortilla and top with feta cheese, tomatoes, and olives.

Ingredients:

-1 whole wheat tortilla

-1/4 cup hummus

-1/4 cup feta cheese, crumbled

-1/4 cup diced tomatoes

-1/4 cup sliced olives

Preparation Method:

-Spread hummus onto tortilla.

-Top with feta cheese, tomatoes, and olives.

-Fold tortilla in half and cook in a skillet over medium heat for 2-3 minutes per side.

Prep Time: 10 minutes

7. Fruit Salad: Create a delicious and healthy fruit salad for a quick snack. Combine your favorite fruit, such as oranges, strawberries, and blueberries. Top with a sprinkle of chopped nuts for an extra crunch.

Ingredients:

-1 cup diced oranges

-1 cup diced strawberries

-1 cup diced blueberries

-1/4 cup chopped nuts

Preparation Method:

-Combine oranges, strawberries, and blueberries in a bowl.

-Top with chopped nuts.

Prep Time: 10 minutes

8. Avocado Toast: Avocado toast is a popular snack that's easy to make. Spread mashed avocado on whole wheat toast and top with a sprinkle of sea salt and red pepper flakes.

Ingredients:

-2 slices whole wheat bread

-1 avocado, mashed

-Sea salt, to taste

-Red pepper flakes, to taste

Preparation Method:

-Spread mashed avocado onto toast.

-Sprinkle with sea salt and red pepper flakes.

Prep Time: 5 minutes

9. Mediterranean Tuna Salad: This Mediterranean twist on classic tuna salad is a great way to get your protein. Combine canned tuna, diced tomatoes, olives, and feta cheese with a drizzle of olive oil.

Ingredients:

-1 can tuna, drained

-1/4 cup diced tomatoes

-1/4 cup sliced olives

-1/4 cup feta cheese, crumbled

-2 tablespoons olive oil

Preparation Method:

-Combine tuna, tomatoes, olives, and feta cheese in a bowl.

-Drizzle with olive oil and mix to combine.

Prep Time: 10 minutes

10. Roasted Chickpeas: Roasted chickpeas are a crunchy and flavorful snack. Toss cooked chickpeas with olive oil, garlic powder, and sea salt. Roast in the oven until crispy.

Ingredients:

-1 can chickpeas, rinsed and drained

-2 tablespoons olive oil

-1 teaspoon garlic powder

-1 teaspoon sea salt

Preparation Method:

-Preheat oven to 400°F.

-Toss chickpeas with olive oil, garlic powder, and sea salt.

-Spread chickpeas onto a baking sheet and roast for 25-30 minutes, stirring occasionally.

Prep Time: 35 minutes

Ben Georg

Smoothies

Mediterranean diet is a way of eating that's based on the traditional dietary habits of people living in the Mediterranean regions. It's characterized by an abundance of fresh fruits and vegetables, whole grains, nuts, fish and olive oil, as well as a moderate consumption of red wine and dairy. Here are 10 delicious and nutritious smoothie recipes that follow a Mediterranean diet.

1. Peach Coconut Smoothie: This smoothie is a refreshing and fruity treat that's perfect for a summer day. It contains peaches, banana, coconut milk, honey, and a pinch of cinnamon. Prep Time: 5 minutes.

Ingredients:

1 ripe peach, peeled and chopped

1 ripe banana, peeled and chopped

1 cup coconut milk

2 tablespoons honey

Pinch of ground cinnamon

Instructions:

1. Place all the ingredients in a blender and blend until smooth.

2. Pour into 2 glasses and enjoy.

2. Kale and Blueberry Smoothie: This smoothie is packed with nutrients and antioxidants thanks to the blueberries and kale. It also contains

banana, Greek yogurt, and almond milk. Prep Time: 5 minutes.

Ingredients:

1 cup kale leaves, stems removed

1/2 cup blueberries

1 ripe banana, peeled and chopped

1/2 cup Greek yogurt

1/2 cup almond milk

Instructions:

1. Place all the ingredients in a blender and blend until smooth.

2. Pour into 2 glasses and enjoy.

3. Avocado and Mango Smoothie: This smoothie is creamy and sweet thanks to the combination of avocado, banana, mango, and honey. Prep Time: 5 minutes.

Ingredients:

1/2 ripe avocado, peeled and chopped

1 ripe banana, peeled and chopped

1/2 cup mango, peeled and chopped

2 tablespoons honey

1/2 cup almond milk

Instructions:

1. Place all the ingredients in a blender and blend until smooth.

2. Pour into 2 glasses and enjoy.

4. Spinach and Pineapple Smoothie: This smoothie is an excellent way to get your daily intake of greens and vitamins. It contains spinach, pineapple, banana, and Greek yogurt. Prep Time: 5 minutes.

Ingredients:

1 cup spinach leaves

1/2 cup pineapple, peeled and chopped

1 ripe banana, peeled and chopped

1/2 cup Greek yogurt

1/2 cup almond milk

Instructions:

1. Place all the ingredients in a blender and blend until smooth.

2. Pour into 2 glasses and enjoy.

5. Apple and Beet Smoothie: This smoothie is full of vitamins and minerals thanks to the combination of apples, beets, and carrots. It also contains banana and almond milk. Prep Time: 5 minutes.

Ingredients:

1/2 cup apples, peeled and chopped

1/2 cup beets, peeled and chopped

1/2 cup carrots, peeled and chopped

1 ripe banana, peeled and chopped

1/2 cup almond milk

Instructions:

1. Place all the ingredients in a blender and blend until smooth.

2. Pour into 2 glasses and enjoy.

6. Cucumber and Orange Smoothie: This smoothie is a great way to get your daily intake of vitamin C and fiber. It contains cucumber, orange, banana, honey, and almond milk. Prep Time: 5 minutes.

Ingredients:

1/2 cup cucumber, peeled and chopped

1/2 cup orange, peeled and chopped

1 ripe banana, peeled and chopped

2 tablespoons honey

1/2 cup almond milk

Instructions:

1. Place all the ingredients in a blender and blend until smooth.

2. Pour into 2 glasses and enjoy.

7. Watermelon and Kiwi Smoothie: This smoothie is packed with vitamins and minerals thanks to the combination of watermelon, kiwi, and banana. Prep Time: 5 minutes.

Ingredients:

1/2 cup watermelon, peeled and chopped

1/2 cup kiwi, peeled and chopped

1 ripe banana, peeled and chopped

1/2 cup almond milk

Instructions:

1. Place all the ingredients in a blender and blend until smooth.

2. Pour into 2 glasses and enjoy.

8. Avocado and Banana Smoothie: This smoothie is creamy and sweet thanks to the combination of avocado and banana. It also

contains honey, Greek yogurt, and almond milk. Prep Time: 5 minutes.

Ingredients:

1/2 ripe avocado, peeled and chopped

1 ripe banana, peeled and chopped

2 tablespoons honey

1/2 cup Greek yogurt

1/2 cup almond milk

Instructions:

1. Place all the ingredients in a blender and blend until smooth.

2. Pour into 2 glasses and enjoy.

9. Chocolate and Banana Smoothie: This smoothie is a great way to satisfy your sweet tooth without compromising your health. It contains banana, cocoa powder, honey, and almond milk. Prep Time: 5 minutes.

Ingredients:

1 ripe banana, peeled and chopped

2 tablespoons cocoa powder

2 tablespoons honey

1/2 cup almond milk

Instructions:

1. Place all the ingredients in a blender and blend until smooth.

2. Pour into 2 glasses and enjoy.

10. Strawberry and Coconut Smoothie: This smoothie is a refreshing and fruity treat thanks to the combination of strawberries, coconut milk, and honey. Prep Time: 5 minutes.

Ingredients:

1 cup strawberries, stemmed and chopped

1 cup coconut milk

2 tablespoons honey

Instructions:

1. Place all the ingredients in a blender and blend until smooth.

2. Pour into 2 glasses and enjoy.

Dessert:

1. Baked Honey-Lemon Baklava: This classic Mediterranean dessert is made with a combination of sweet honey and tart lemon, and is sure to please any dessert lover. Ingredients include walnuts, butter, honey, lemon juice, sugar, phyllo dough, and cinnamon. Preparation time is about 45 minutes.

2. Greek Yogurt Cake: This light and creamy cake is a delicious way to satisfy your sweet tooth while still eating healthy. Ingredients include Greek yogurt, butter, sugar, eggs, all-purpose flour, baking powder, and vanilla extract. Preparation time is about 25 minutes.

3. Fig and Honey Tart: This dessert is as delicious as it is beautiful. Fresh figs, honey, puff pastry, and a sprinkling of cinnamon make this tart a must-try. Ingredients include puff pastry, fresh figs, honey, and cinnamon. Preparation time is about 30 minutes.

4. Orange and Almond Cake: This sweet and citrusy cake is the perfect end to any meal. Ingredients include almond meal, orange zest, eggs, sugar, orange juice, and baking powder. Preparation time is about 40 minutes.

5. Honey and Date Cake: This dessert is a great way to get your sweet fix without feeling guilty. Ingredients include dates, walnuts, honey, eggs, sugar, and baking powder. Preparation time is about 35 minutes.

6. Olive Oil and Honey Cake: Olive oil and honey make this cake extra moist and delicious. Ingredients include olive oil, honey, eggs, sugar, all-purpose flour, baking powder, and vanilla extract. Preparation time is about 40 minutes.

7. Baklava Cheesecake: This decadent dessert combines the best of both worlds – the crunchiness of baklava and the creaminess of cheesecake. Ingredients include walnuts, butter, honey, cream cheese, eggs, sugar, phyllo dough, and cinnamon. Preparation time is about 45 minutes.

8. Carrot and Walnut Cake: This moist and flavorful cake is a great way to enjoy vegetables

in a dessert. Ingredients include carrots, walnuts, butter, eggs, sugar, all-purpose flour, cinnamon, and baking powder. Preparation time is about 45 minutes.

9. Fig and Walnut Tart: This tart is a great way to enjoy the sweet flavor of figs without having to make a whole cake. Ingredients include puff pastry, fresh figs, walnuts, honey, and cinnamon. Preparation time is about 30 minutes.

10. Greek Yogurt Parfait: This is a great way to satisfy your sweet tooth without overindulging. Ingredients include Greek yogurt, honey, and your favorite toppings, such as fresh fruit or nuts. Preparation time is about 10 minutes.

Resources for Mediterranean diet

The Mediterranean diet is one of the healthiest diets to follow and has been linked to various benefits such as reduced risk of chronic diseases, improved heart health, and weight loss. For those who must follow a gluten-free diet, the Mediterranean diet can still be an excellent choice. There are many resources available to help you stick to a gluten-free Mediterranean diet.

One of the best resources is a gluten-free Mediterranean diet cookbook. Cookbooks provide delicious and easy-to-make recipes that adhere to the gluten-free Mediterranean diet guidelines. Look for cookbooks that focus on ingredients that are naturally gluten-free, such as vegetables, fruits, nuts, legumes, and healthy fats.

In addition to cookbooks, there are a variety of websites and blogs that specialize in gluten-free Mediterranean diet recipes. Many of these sites will provide recipes for breakfast, lunch, and dinner, as well as snacks and desserts. Many of these recipes can be tailored to meet individual dietary needs and preferences.

A registered dietitian (RD) can also be an invaluable resource for those who want to follow a gluten-free Mediterranean diet. An RD can help create a personalized meal plan that meets your individual needs and preferences. They can also provide guidance on how to read labels and identify hidden sources of gluten.

Finally, there are several organizations and support groups dedicated to helping people follow a gluten-free Mediterranean diet. These groups can provide valuable resources and advice on sticking to the diet. They can also be a great source of support and encouragement.

By taking advantage of these resources, you can easily follow a gluten-free Mediterranean diet and enjoy all the health benefits it has to offer.

Ben Georg

Appetizer and snacks

Vegetarian appetizer and snacks:

1. Mediterranean Roasted Vegetable Platter: Roast colorful vegetables like peppers, onions, carrots, and eggplant and serve with a tangy tahini sauce.

2. Hummus and Crudite: Serve a variety of raw vegetables with a creamy, rich hummus dip.

3. Baked Eggplant Fries: Cut eggplant into strips, coat with olive oil, and bake in a preheated oven. Serve with a yogurt-based dip.

4. Mediterranean Spinach Pies: Wrap a spiced spinach mixture in gluten-free pastry dough and bake until golden. Serve warm or cold.

5. Tomato and Mozzarella Skewers: Thread cherry tomatoes and mozzarella cubes onto skewers and drizzle with olive oil and balsamic vinegar.

6. Zucchini Fritters: Shred zucchini and mix with eggs, herbs, and cheese. Fry in a shallow pan until golden. Serve with a yogurt-based dip.

7. Roasted Red Pepper and Feta Dip: Blend roasted red peppers, feta cheese, olive oil, and garlic together in a food processor and serve with gluten-free crackers.

8. Mediterranean Flatbread: Spread a gluten-free flatbread with pesto and top with sliced tomatoes, olives, and feta cheese. Bake until the cheese melts.

9. Stuffed Peppers: Core bell peppers and fill with a mixture of cooked rice, vegetables, and herbs. Bake until the peppers are tender.

10. Zucchini Noodles with Pesto: Spiralize zucchini and combine with pesto and sun-dried tomatoes. Serve over cooked quinoa for an extra boost of protein.

Sea food appetizer and snacks:

1. Avocado and Shrimp Salad: This gluten-free Mediterranean appetizer takes only 10 minutes to prepare. Peel and devein 1 pound of shrimp and cook in boiling water, then cool and set aside. Slice 2 avocados, 1/2 red onion, 1/2 cup of cherry tomatoes, and a handful of fresh cilantro. Place all ingredients in a medium bowl and add the cooked shrimp. Drizzle with olive oil, lemon juice, and season with salt and pepper to taste.

2. Olive Tapenade: This classic Mediterranean appetizer is easy to prepare and only takes 10 minutes. Combine 1/2 cup of pitted black olives, 1/4 cup of olive oil, 1 clove of garlic, and 2 tablespoons of capers in a food processor

and pulse until it forms a paste. Serve with slices of crusty gluten-free baguette or crackers.

3. Hummus with Pita Chips: This gluten-free Mediterranean snack is ready in 15 minutes. In a food processor, blend 2 cups of cooked chickpeas (garbanzo beans), 2 tablespoons of tahini, 1/4 cup of olive oil, 2 cloves of garlic, 2 tablespoons of lemon juice, and salt to taste. Serve with homemade pita chips. Slice gluten-free pita bread into wedges, brush with olive oil, sprinkle with sea salt, and bake at 375 degrees Fahrenheit for 10 minutes.

4. Grilled Calamari: This gluten-free Mediterranean snack takes about 10 minutes to prepare and cook. Marinate 1 pound of squid in lemon juice, olive oil, garlic, and herbs. Thread

squid on skewers and grill for 5 minutes, turning once. Serve with lemon wedges and a simple salad.

5. Mediterranean Flatbread: This gluten-free Mediterranean snack takes about 10 minutes to prepare. Preheat oven to 350 degrees Fahrenheit. Cut a gluten-free flatbread into 8 pieces and top with feta cheese, black olives, and fresh oregano. Bake for 8 minutes or until cheese is melted.

6. Grilled Octopus: This gluten-free Mediterranean snack takes about 15 minutes to prepare and cook. Marinate 1 pound of cleaned octopus in olive oil, garlic, lemon juice, and herbs. Grill for 5 minutes, turning once. Serve with lemon wedges and a simple salad.

7. Shrimp Cocktail: This gluten-free Mediterranean snack takes about 10 minutes to prepare. Peel and devein 1 pound of shrimp and cook in boiling water. Cool and serve with a spicy cocktail sauce.

8. Mediterranean Stuffed Mushrooms: This gluten-free Mediterranean snack takes about 15 minutes to prepare and cook. Clean 1/2 pound of mushrooms and remove stems. Stuff mushroom caps with a mixture of 1/2 cup of crumbled feta cheese and 1/4 cup of chopped fresh parsley. Top with a drizzle of olive oil and bake at 375 degrees Fahrenheit for 10 minutes.

9. Baked Zucchini Fritters: This gluten-free Mediterranean snack takes about 20 minutes to

prepare and cook. Grate 2 zucchini, 1 onion, and 2 cloves of garlic. Mix in an egg, 1/4 cup of gluten-free bread crumbs, 1/4 cup of grated Parmesan cheese, and a pinch of salt and pepper. Form into small patties and bake at 375 degrees Fahrenheit for 10 minutes.

10. Eggplant and Tomato Crostini: This gluten-free Mediterranean snack takes about 15 minutes to prepare. Slice 1 eggplant into 1/4-inch thick slices and bake at 375 degrees Fahrenheit for 10 minutes. While the eggplant is baking, slice a baguette into slices and brush with olive oil. Toast in the oven for 5 minutes. Top with roasted eggplant slices, chopped tomatoes, and basil leaves. Drizzle with balsamic glaze and serve warm.

Meat appetizers and snacks

1. Greek-Style Grilled Chicken Skewers: Marinate chicken cubes with olive oil, garlic, oregano, and lemon juice then thread the chicken onto skewers and grill until cooked through. Prep time: 10 minutes.

2. Grilled Lamb Kebabs: Marinate cubes of lamb with garlic, oregano, mint, and olive oil. Thread the cubes onto skewers and grill until cooked through. Prep time: 10 minutes.

1. Greek-Style Grilled Chicken Skewers: Marinate chicken cubes with olive oil, garlic, oregano, and lemon juice then thread the chicken onto skewers and grill until cooked through. Prep time: 10 minutes.

2. Grilled Lamb Kebabs: Marinate cubes of lamb with garlic, oregano, mint, and olive oil. Thread the cubes onto skewers and grill until cooked through. Prep time: 10 minutes.

3. Zucchini Fritters: Shred zucchini, mix with eggs and your choice of herbs, form into small flat patties, and fry in olive oil until golden brown. Prep time: 10 minutes.

4. Baked Feta Cheese: Place feta cheese in an oven-safe dish, top with olive oil, oregano, and thyme, and bake until cheese is melted and golden. Prep time: 10 minutes.

5. Mediterranean Meatballs: Combine ground beef, feta cheese, garlic, oregano, and parsley. Form into small balls and fry in olive oil until cooked through. Prep time: 10 minutes.

6. Prosciutto-Wrapped Asparagus: Wrap asparagus spears with prosciutto, drizzle with olive oil, and bake until the prosciutto is crisp. Prep time: 10 minutes.

7. Grilled Lamb Chops: Marinate lamb chops with garlic, oregano, and olive oil. Grill until cooked through. Prep time: 10 minutes.

8. Spanish-Style Meatballs: Combine ground beef, garlic, oregano, parsley, and paprika.

Form into small balls and fry in olive oil until cooked through. Prep time: 10 minutes.

9. Italian-Style Sausage Skewers: Marinate Italian sausage cubes with garlic, oregano, and olive oil. Thread the cubes onto skewers and grill until cooked through. Prep time: 10 minutes.

10. Spicy Shrimp Skewers: Marinate shrimp cubes with garlic, chili peppers, and olive oil. Thread the cubes onto skewers and grill until cooked through. Prep time: 10 minutes.

Soups and salad

Vegetarian soup and salad:

1. Fennel, Orange, & Avocado Salad: Prep time: 10 minutes. This gluten-free salad is light and refreshing, and it features a beautiful combination of flavors. To prepare, combine 4 cups of thinly sliced fennel, 2 peeled and segmented oranges, a diced avocado, and ¼ cup of fresh chopped basil in a bowl. In a separate bowl, whisk together ¼ cup of extra-virgin olive oil, 2 tablespoons of fresh lemon juice, and 1 teaspoon of honey. Pour the dressing over the salad and toss to combine.

2. Roasted Red Pepper & Tomato Soup: Prep time: 25 minutes. This flavorful soup is perfect for a gluten-free Mediterranean diet. To

prepare, preheat the oven to 400 degrees Fahrenheit. Place 2 large red bell peppers and 1 pint of cherry tomatoes on a baking sheet. Drizzle the vegetables with 2 tablespoons of olive oil, sprinkle with salt and pepper, and roast in the oven for 15 minutes. Transfer the roasted vegetables to a blender and add 2 cups of vegetable stock, 2 cloves of garlic, and a pinch of red pepper flakes. Blend until smooth and then season with additional salt and pepper if necessary.

3. Mediterranean Orzo Salad: Prep time: 15 minutes. This gluten-free orzo salad is packed with flavor and texture. To prepare, cook 1 cup of orzo according to the package instructions. In a large bowl, combine the cooked orzo with 1 cup of diced tomatoes, 1 cup of diced cucumber, ½ cup of crumbled feta cheese, ½

cup of sliced olives, ¼ cup of chopped fresh parsley, and ¼ cup of chopped fresh mint. In a separate bowl, whisk together 3 tablespoons of extra-virgin olive oil, 2 tablespoons of red wine vinegar, and 1 teaspoon of honey. Pour the dressing over the salad and toss to combine.

4. Spinach & Chickpea Soup: Prep time: 20 minutes. This hearty soup is perfect for a gluten-free Mediterranean diet. To prepare, heat 2 tablespoons of olive oil in a large pot over medium-high heat. Add 1 diced onion, 2 cloves of minced garlic, and 2 teaspoons of ground cumin. Cook until the vegetables are softened, about 5 minutes. Add 1 can of chickpeas (drained and rinsed), 5 cups of vegetable stock, and 2 cups of baby spinach leaves. Bring the mixture to a boil, reduce the heat to low, and simmer for 15 minutes.

5. Mediterranean Quinoa Salad: Prep time: 10 minutes. This gluten-free quinoa salad is loaded with flavor and texture. To prepare, cook 1 cup of quinoa according to the package instructions. In a large bowl, combine the cooked quinoa with 1 diced red bell pepper, 1 diced cucumber, ½ cup of crumbled feta cheese, ½ cup of chopped fresh parsley, ¼ cup of sliced olives, and ¼ cup of chopped fresh mint. In a separate bowl, whisk together 3 tablespoons of extra-virgin olive oil, 2 tablespoons of red wine vinegar, and 1 teaspoon of honey. Pour the dressing over the salad and toss to combine.

6. Lentil Soup: Prep time: 25 minutes. This hearty soup is perfect for a gluten-free Mediterranean diet. To prepare, heat 2 tablespoons of olive oil in a large pot over

medium-high heat. Add 1 diced onion, 2 cloves of minced garlic, and 1 teaspoon of ground cumin. Cook until the vegetables are softened, about 5 minutes. Add 1 cup of dried lentils, 5 cups of vegetable stock, and 1 bay leaf. Bring the mixture to a boil, reduce the heat to low, and simmer for 20 minutes.

7. Kale & White Bean Salad: Prep time: 10 minutes. This gluten-free salad is packed with flavor and nutrition. To prepare, combine 4 cups of chopped kale, one 15-ounce can of white beans (drained and rinsed), 1 diced red bell pepper, ¼ cup of crumbled feta cheese, and ¼ cup of chopped fresh parsley in a bowl. In a separate bowl, whisk together 3 tablespoons of extra-virgin olive oil, 2 tablespoons of red wine vinegar, 1 teaspoon of honey, and a pinch of

salt and pepper. Pour the dressing over the salad and toss to combine.

8. Roasted Eggplant Soup: Prep time: 25 minutes. This flavorful soup is perfect for a gluten-free Mediterranean diet. To prepare, preheat the oven to 400 degrees Fahrenheit. Place 2 large eggplants on a baking sheet and drizzle with 2 tablespoons of olive oil. Sprinkle with salt and pepper and roast in the oven for 20 minutes. Transfer the roasted eggplants to a blender and add 2 cups of vegetable stock, 2 cloves of garlic, and a pinch of red pepper flakes. Blend until smooth and then season with additional salt and pepper if necessary.

9. Greek Salad: Prep time: 10 minutes. This gluten-free salad is a classic Mediterranean

dish. To prepare, combine 5 cups of chopped romaine lettuce, 1 diced cucumber, 1 diced red onion, 1 diced tomato, ½ cup of crumbled feta cheese, and ½ cup of pitted kalamata olives in a bowl. In a separate bowl, whisk together 3 tablespoons of extra-virgin olive oil, 2 tablespoons of red wine vinegar, and 1 teaspoon of honey. Pour the dressing over the salad and toss to combine.

10. Mushroom & Tomato Risotto: Prep time: 25 minutes. This gluten-free risotto is a delicious and comforting dish. To prepare, heat 2 tablespoons of olive oil in a large pot over medium-high heat. Add 1 diced onion, 2 cloves of minced garlic, and 1 cup of sliced mushrooms. Cook until the vegetables are softened, about 5 minutes. Add 1 cup of Arborio rice, 5 cups of vegetable stock, and 1

cup of diced tomatoes. Bring the mixture to a boil, reduce the heat to low, and simmer for 20 minutes.

Seafood soups and salad

1. Mediterranean Shrimp and Bean Soup:

Prep Time: 20 minutes

Ingredients:

- 2 tablespoons olive oil

- 1 onion, diced

- 2 cloves garlic, minced

- 2 carrots, peeled and diced

- 2 celery stalks, diced

- 2 teaspoons dried oregano

- 2 teaspoons ground cumin

- 1 teaspoon smoked paprika

- 1/2 teaspoon sea salt

- 1 (14.5-ounce) can diced tomatoes

- 4 cups vegetable broth

- 1 (15-ounce) can cannellini beans, drained and rinsed

- 1 pound large shrimp, peeled and deveined

- 2 tablespoons freshly chopped parsley

- Juice of 1/2 lemon

Instructions:

Heat the olive oil in a large pot over medium heat. Add the onion, garlic, carrots, and celery and sauté for 5-6 minutes, until softened.

Add the oregano, cumin, smoked paprika, and salt and sauté for another minute.

Add the diced tomatoes, vegetable broth, and cannellini beans and bring to a boil. Reduce the heat to low and simmer for 10 minutes.

Add the shrimp and continue to simmer for another 5 minutes, until the shrimp are cooked through.

Add the parsley and lemon juice. Taste and adjust seasonings, if desired.

Serve warm.

2. Mediterranean Tuna Salad:

Prep Time: 10 minutes

Ingredients:

- 2 (5-ounce) cans tuna in olive oil, drained

- 1/2 cup diced cucumber

- 1/2 cup diced red bell pepper

- 1/2 cup diced tomatoes

- 1/4 cup sliced olives

- 2 tablespoons chopped fresh parsley

- 2 tablespoons extra-virgin olive oil

- Juice of 1/2 lemon

- Salt and pepper, to taste

Instructions:

In a medium bowl, combine the tuna, cucumber, bell pepper, tomatoes, olives, and parsley.

Add the olive oil, lemon juice, salt, and pepper and mix until combined.

Serve over a bed of greens or in a gluten-free wrap.

3. Mediterranean Cod Soup:

Prep Time: 20 minutes

Ingredients:

- 2 tablespoons olive oil

- 1 onion, diced

- 2 cloves garlic, minced

- 2 carrots, peeled and diced

- 2 celery stalks, diced

- 2 teaspoons dried oregano

- 2 teaspoons ground cumin

- 1 teaspoon smoked paprika

- 1/2 teaspoon sea salt

- 1 (14.5-ounce) can diced tomatoes

- 4 cups vegetable broth

- 1 pound cod fillets, cut into 1-inch pieces

- 2 tablespoons freshly chopped parsley

- Juice of 1/2 lemon

Instructions:

Heat the olive oil in a large pot over medium heat. Add the onion, garlic, carrots, and celery and sauté for 5-6 minutes, until softened.

Add the oregano, cumin, smoked paprika, and salt and sauté for another minute.

Add the diced tomatoes, vegetable broth, and cod and bring to a boil. Reduce the heat to low and simmer for 10 minutes.

Add the parsley and lemon juice. Taste and adjust seasonings, if desired.

Serve warm.

4. Mediterranean Salmon Salad:

Prep Time: 10 minutes

Ingredients:

- 2 (5-ounce) cans wild-caught salmon, drained

- 1/2 cup diced cucumber

- 1/2 cup diced red bell pepper

- 1/2 cup diced tomatoes

- 1/4 cup sliced olives

- 2 tablespoons chopped fresh parsley

- 2 tablespoons extra-virgin olive oil

- Juice of 1/2 lemon

- Salt and pepper, to taste

Instructions:

In a medium bowl, combine the salmon, cucumber, bell pepper, tomatoes, olives, and parsley.

Add the olive oil, lemon juice, salt, and pepper and mix until combined.

Serve over a bed of greens or in a gluten-free wrap.

5. Mediterranean Mussel Soup:

Prep Time: 20 minutes

Ingredients:

- 2 tablespoons olive oil

- 1 onion, diced

- 2 cloves garlic, minced

- 2 carrots, peeled and diced

- 2 celery stalks, diced

- 2 teaspoons dried oregano

- 2 teaspoons ground cumin

- 1 teaspoon smoked paprika

- 1/2 teaspoon sea salt

- 1 (14.5-ounce) can diced tomatoes

- 4 cups vegetable broth

- 1 pound mussels, scrubbed and debearded

- 2 tablespoons freshly chopped parsley

- Juice of 1/2 lemon

Instructions:

Heat the olive oil in a large pot over medium heat. Add the onion, garlic, carrots, and celery and sauté for 5-6 minutes, until softened.

Add the oregano, cumin, smoked paprika, and salt and sauté for another minute.

Add the diced tomatoes, vegetable broth, and mussels and bring to a boil. Reduce the heat to low and simmer for 10 minutes, until the mussels are cooked through.

Add the parsley and lemon juice. Taste and adjust seasonings, if desired.

Serve warm.

6. Mediterranean Octopus Salad:

Prep Time: 10 minutes

Ingredients:

- 2 (5-ounce) cans octopus, drained

- 1/2 cup diced cucumber

- 1/2 cup diced red bell pepper

- 1/2 cup diced tomatoes

- 1/4 cup sliced olives

- 2 tablespoons chopped fresh parsley

- 2 tablespoons extra-virgin olive oil

- Juice of 1/2 lemon

- Salt and pepper, to taste

Instructions:

In a medium bowl, combine the octopus, cucumber, bell pepper, tomatoes, olives, and parsley.

Add the olive oil, lemon juice, salt, and pepper and mix until combined.

Serve over a bed of greens or in a gluten-free wrap.

7. Mediterranean Crab Soup:

Prep Time: 20 minutes

Ingredients:

- 2 tablespoons olive oil

- 1 onion, diced

- 2 cloves garlic, minced

- 2 carrots, peeled and diced

- 2 celery stalks, diced

- 2 teaspoons dried oregano

- 2 teaspoons ground cumin

- 1 teaspoon smoked paprika

- 1/2 teaspoon sea salt

- 1 (14.5-ounce) can diced tomatoes

- 4 cups vegetable broth

- 1 pound crabmeat, picked over

- 2 tablespoons freshly chopped parsley

- Juice of 1/2 lemon

Instructions:

Heat the olive oil in a large pot over medium heat. Add the onion, garlic, carrots, and celery and sauté for 5-6 minutes, until softened.

Add the oregano, cumin, smoked paprika, and salt and sauté for another minute.

Add the diced tomatoes, vegetable broth, and crabmeat and bring to a boil. Reduce the heat to low and simmer for 10 minutes.

Add the parsley and lemon juice. Taste and adjust seasonings, if desired.

Serve warm.

8. Mediterranean Clam Soup:

Prep Time: 20 minutes

Ingredients:

- 2 tablespoons olive oil

- 1 onion, diced

- 2 cloves garlic, minced

- 2 carrots, peeled and diced

- 2 celery stalks, diced

- 2 teaspoons dried oregano

- 2 teaspoons ground cumin

- 1 teaspoon smoked paprika

- 1/2 teaspoon sea salt

- 1 (14.5-ounce) can diced tomatoes

- 4 cups vegetable broth

- 1 pound clams, scrubbed

- 2 tablespoons freshly chopped parsley

- Juice of 1/2 lemon

Instructions:

Heat the olive oil in a large pot over medium heat. Add the onion, garlic, carrots, and celery and sauté for 5-6 minutes, until softened.

Add the oregano, cumin, smoked paprika, and salt and sauté for another minute.

Add the diced tomatoes, vegetable broth, and clams and bring to a boil. Reduce the heat to low and simmer for 10 minutes, until the clams are cooked through.

Add the parsley and lemon juice. Taste and adjust seasonings, if desired.

Serve warm.

9. Mediterranean Squid Salad:

Prep Time: 10 minutes

Ingredients:

- 2 (5-ounce) cans squid, drained

- 1/2 cup diced cucumber

- 1/2 cup diced red bell pepper

- 1/2 cup diced tomatoes

- 1/4 cup sliced olives

- 2 tablespoons chopped fresh parsley

- 2 tablespoons extra-virgin olive oil

- Juice of 1/2 lemon

- Salt and pepper, to taste

Instructions:

In a medium bowl, combine the squid, cucumber, bell pepper, tomatoes, olives, and parsley.

Add the olive oil, lemon juice, salt, and pepper and mix until combined.

Serve over a bed of greens or in a gluten-free wrap.

10. Mediterranean Scallop Salad:

Prep Time: 10 minutes

Ingredients:

- 2 (5-ounce) cans scallops, drained

- 1/2 cup diced cucumber

- 1/2 cup diced red bell pepper

- 1/2 cup diced tomatoes

- 1/4 cup sliced olives

- 2 tablespoons chopped fresh parsley

- 2 tablespoons extra-virgin olive oil

- Juice of 1/2 lemon

- Salt and pepper, to taste

Instructions:

In a medium bowl, combine the scallops, cucumber, bell pepper, tomatoes, olives, and parsley.

Add the olive oil, lemon juice, salt, and pepper and mix until combined.

Serve over a bed of greens or in a gluten-free wrap.

Meat soups and salad

1. Mediterranean Lamb Soup – Prep Time: 15 minutes

Ingredients: 2 tablespoons olive oil, 1 onion, finely chopped, 1 carrot, finely chopped, 2 garlic cloves, minced, 1 teaspoon ground cumin, 1 teaspoon ground coriander, 1/4 teaspoon ground cinnamon, 1/4 teaspoon ground allspice, 2 pounds boneless lamb, cubed, 4 cups chicken broth, 1 (14-ounce) can diced tomatoes, 2 cups cooked chickpeas, 1 cup cooked white or brown rice, 1/4 cup chopped fresh parsley

Instructions:

a. Heat the olive oil in a large pot over medium heat.

b. Add the onion and carrot and cook until softened, about 5 minutes.

c. Add the garlic and spices and cook until fragrant, about 1 minute.

d. Add the lamb and cook until browned, about 5 minutes.

e. Add the chicken broth, tomatoes, chickpeas, and rice and bring to a boil.

f. Reduce the heat to low and simmer for 10 minutes.

g. Stir in the parsley and season with salt and pepper.

h. Serve hot.

2. Mediterranean Shrimp Soup – Prep Time: 10 minutes

Ingredients: 2 tablespoons olive oil, 1 onion, finely chopped, 1 red bell pepper, seeded and finely chopped, 2 garlic cloves, minced, 1 teaspoon ground cumin, 1 teaspoon smoked paprika, 1/4 teaspoon ground turmeric, 1/4 teaspoon ground cinnamon, 1/4 teaspoon ground allspice, 1/4 teaspoon cayenne pepper, 1 pound raw shrimp, peeled and deveined, 4 cups chicken broth, 1 (14-ounce) can diced tomatoes, 1 cup cooked white or brown rice, 1/4 cup chopped fresh parsley

Instructions:

a. Heat the olive oil in a large pot over medium heat.

b. Add the onion and bell pepper and cook until softened, about 5 minutes.

c. Add the garlic and spices and cook until fragrant, about 1 minute.

d. Add the shrimp and cook until pink, about 3 minutes.

e. Add the chicken broth, tomatoes, and rice and bring to a boil.

f. Reduce the heat to low and simmer for 5 minutes.

g. Stir in the parsley and season with salt and pepper.

h. Serve hot.

3. Mediterranean Chicken Soup – Prep Time: 15 minutes

Ingredients: 2 tablespoons olive oil, 1 onion, finely chopped, 1 carrot, finely chopped, 2 garlic cloves, minced, 1 teaspoon ground cumin, 1 teaspoon ground coriander, 1/4 teaspoon ground cinnamon, 1/4 teaspoon ground allspice, 2 pounds boneless chicken, cubed, 4 cups chicken broth, 1 (14-ounce) can diced tomatoes, 2 cups cooked chickpeas, 1 cup cooked white or brown rice, 1/4 cup chopped fresh parsley

Instructions:

a. Heat the olive oil in a large pot over medium heat.

b. Add the onion and carrot and cook until softened, about 5 minutes.

c. Add the garlic and spices and cook until fragrant, about 1 minute.

d. Add the chicken and cook until browned, about 5 minutes.

e. Add the chicken broth, tomatoes, chickpeas, and rice and bring to a boil.

f. Reduce the heat to low and simmer for 10 minutes.

g. Stir in the parsley and season with salt and pepper.

h. Serve hot.

4. Mediterranean Beef Soup – Prep Time: 15 minutes

Ingredients: 2 tablespoons olive oil, 1 onion, finely chopped, 1 carrot, finely chopped, 2 garlic cloves, minced, 1 teaspoon ground cumin, 1 teaspoon ground coriander, 1/4 teaspoon ground cinnamon, 1/4 teaspoon ground allspice, 2 pounds beef, cubed, 4 cups beef broth, 1 (14-ounce) can diced tomatoes, 2 cups cooked chickpeas, 1 cup cooked white or brown rice, 1/4 cup chopped fresh parsley

Instructions:

a. Heat the olive oil in a large pot over medium heat.

b. Add the onion and carrot and cook until softened, about 5 minutes.

c. Add the garlic and spices and cook until fragrant, about 1 minute.

d. Add the beef and cook until browned, about 5 minutes.

e. Add the beef broth, tomatoes, chickpeas, and rice and bring to a boil.

f. Reduce the heat to low and simmer for 10 minutes.

g. Stir in the parsley and season with salt and pepper.

h. Serve hot.

5. Mediterranean Tuna Salad – Prep Time: 10 minutes

Ingredients: 2 cans tuna, drained and flaked, 1/4 cup diced red onion, 1/4 cup sliced kalamata olives, 1/4 cup diced red bell pepper, 1/4 cup diced cucumber, 1/4 cup diced tomatoes, 2 tablespoons capers, 2 tablespoons olive oil, 1 tablespoon red wine vinegar, 1 teaspoon dried oregano, 1/4 teaspoon sea salt, 1/4 teaspoon ground black pepper

Instructions:

a. In a medium bowl, combine the tuna, red onion, olives, bell pepper, cucumber, tomatoes, and capers.

b. In a small bowl, whisk together the olive oil, red wine vinegar, oregano, salt, and pepper.

c. Pour the dressing over the tuna mixture and stir to combine.

d. Serve chilled or at room temperature.

6. Mediterranean Egg Salad – Prep Time: 10 minutes

Ingredients: 4 hard boiled eggs, peeled and diced, 1/4 cup diced red onion, 1/4 cup diced celery, 1/4 cup diced red bell pepper, 1/4 cup diced cucumber, 1/4 cup diced tomatoes, 2 tablespoons capers, 2 tablespoons olive oil, 1 tablespoon red wine vinegar, 1 teaspoon dried oregano, 1/4 teaspoon sea salt, 1/4 teaspoon ground black pepper

Instructions:

a. In a medium bowl, combine the eggs, red onion, celery, bell pepper, cucumber, tomatoes, and capers.

b. In a small bowl, whisk together the olive oil, red wine vinegar, oregano, salt, and pepper.

c. Pour the dressing over the egg mixture and stir to combine.

d. Serve chilled or at room temperature.

7. Mediterranean Chicken Salad – Prep Time: 10 minutes

Ingredients: 2 cups cooked chicken, diced, 1/4 cup diced red onion, 1/4 cup sliced kalamata olives, 1/4 cup diced red bell pepper, 1/4 cup diced cucumber, 1/4 cup diced tomatoes, 2 tablespoons capers, 2 tablespoons olive oil, 1 tablespoon red wine vinegar, 1 teaspoon dried oregano, 1/4 teaspoon sea salt, 1/4 teaspoon ground black pepper

Instructions:

a. In a medium bowl, combine the chicken, red onion, olives, bell pepper, cucumber, tomatoes, and capers.

b. In a small bowl, whisk together the olive oil, red wine vinegar, oregano, salt, and pepper.

c. Pour the dressing over the chicken mixture and stir to combine.

d. Serve chilled or at room temperature.

8. Mediterranean Fish Soup – Prep Time: 15 minutes

Ingredients: 2 tablespoons olive oil, 1 onion, finely chopped, 1 carrot, finely chopped, 2 garlic cloves, minced, 1 teaspoon ground cumin, 1 teaspoon ground coriander, 1/4 teaspoon ground cinnamon, 1/4 teaspoon ground allspice, 1 pound white fish, cubed, 4 cups fish broth, 1 (14-ounce) can diced tomatoes, 2 cups cooked chickpeas, 1 cup cooked white or brown rice, 1/4 cup chopped fresh parsley

Instructions:

a. Heat the olive oil in a large pot over medium heat.

b. Add the onion and carrot and cook until softened, about 5 minutes.

c. Add the garlic and spices and cook until fragrant, about 1 minute.

d. Add the fish and cook until browned, about 5 minutes.

e. Add the fish broth, tomatoes, chickpeas, and rice and bring to a boil.

f. Reduce the heat to low and simmer for 10 minutes.

g. Stir in the parsley and season with salt and pepper.

h. Serve hot.

9. Mediterranean Quinoa Salad – Prep Time: 10 minutes

Ingredients: 2 cups cooked quinoa, 1/4 cup diced red onion, 1/4 cup sliced kalamata olives, 1/4 cup diced red bell pepper, 1/4 cup diced cucumber, 1/4 cup diced tomatoes, 2 tablespoons capers, 2 tablespoons olive oil, 1 tablespoon red wine vinegar, 1 teaspoon dried oregano, 1/4 teaspoon sea salt, 1/4 teaspoon ground black pepper

Instructions:

a. In a medium bowl, combine the quinoa, red onion, olives, bell pepper, cucumber, tomatoes, and capers.

b. In a small bowl, whisk together the olive oil, red wine vinegar, oregano, salt, and pepper.

c. Pour the dressing over the quinoa mixture and stir to combine.

d. Serve chilled or at room temperature.

10. Mediterranean Lentil Soup – Prep Time: 15 minutes

Ingredients: 2 tablespoons olive oil, 1 onion, finely chopped, 1 carrot, finely chopped, 2 garlic cloves, minced, 1 teaspoon ground cumin, 1 teaspoon ground coriander, 1/4 teaspoon ground cinnamon, 1/4 teaspoon ground allspice, 1 cup dried lentils, 4 cups vegetable broth, 1 (14-ounce) can diced tomatoes, 2 cups cooked chickpeas, 1 cup cooked white or brown rice, 1/4 cup chopped fresh parsley

Instructions:

a. Heat the olive oil in a large pot over medium heat.

b. Add the onion and carrot and cook until softened, about 5 minutes.

c. Add the garlic and spices and cook until fragrant, about 1 minute.

d. Add the lentils and cook for 1 minute.

e. Add the vegetable broth, tomatoes, chickpeas, and rice and bring to a boil.

f. Reduce the heat to low and simmer for 10 minutes.

g. Stir in the parsley and season with salt and pepper.

h. Serve hot.

Ben Georg

Beverages

Vegetarian beverage:

1. Watermelon Mint Cooler: Blend together 2 cups of chopped watermelon, juice of 1 lime, 2 tablespoons of honey, and a handful of mint leaves. Enjoy chilled. Prep Time: 5 minutes

2. Chia Fresca: Mix 2 tablespoons of chia seeds in a glass of cold water. Add a squeeze of lemon and a teaspoon of honey. Stir and enjoy. Prep Time: 5 minutes

3. Coconut Pineapple Smoothie: Blend together 1 cup of coconut milk, ½ cup of frozen pineapple, and 1 teaspoon of honey. Serve chilled. Prep Time: 7 minutes

4. Cucumber Mint Detox Drink: Blend together 1 cucumber, 1 cup of spinach, 1 teaspoon of lemon juice, and a handful of mint leaves. Enjoy chilled. Prep Time: 5 minutes

5. Green Juice: Blend together 1 cucumber, 1 celery stalk, 1 green apple, 1 cup of spinach, and a handful of parsley. Enjoy chilled. Prep Time: 7 minutes

6. Beetroot and Carrot Juice: Blend together 2 beets, 2 carrots, and 1 apple. Add a squeeze of lemon and honey to taste. Enjoy chilled. Prep Time: 8 minutes

7. Turmeric Milk: Heat 1 cup of unsweetened almond milk in a saucepan. Add 1 teaspoon of turmeric powder, 1 teaspoon of honey, and a pinch of ground black pepper. Cook for a few minutes and enjoy warm. Prep Time: 10 minutes

8. Coconut Water: Open a chilled can of coconut water and enjoy. Prep Time: 2 minutes

9. Herbal Tea: Steep 1 teaspoon of dried herbs (such as chamomile, peppermint, or ginger) in a cup of hot water. Add a teaspoon of honey if desired. Enjoy warm. Prep Time: 5 minutes

10. Green Tea: Steep 1 teaspoon of green tea leaves in a cup of hot water. Add a squeeze of

lemon and honey if desired. Enjoy warm. Prep Time: 5 minutes

Seafood beverage:

1. Grilled Shrimp Cocktail: Preheat the oven to 375 degrees F. Peel and de-vein the shrimp, then place them onto a baking sheet lined with parchment paper. Drizzle with olive oil and season with salt, pepper and garlic powder. Bake for 10 minutes, or until cooked through. Serve in a bowl with cocktail sauce on the side. Prep Time: 10 minutes.

2. Zucchini Noodles with Shrimp: Heat 1 tablespoon olive oil in a large skillet over medium heat. Add 1 cup zucchini noodles, 2 minced garlic cloves, and 1/2 teaspoon dried oregano. Cook for 3 minutes. Add 1/2 cup frozen shrimp and cook for an additional 2 minutes. Season with salt and pepper and serve. Prep Time: 5 minutes.

3. Salmon Ceviche: In a medium bowl, mix together 1/2 pound cooked and flaked salmon, 1/2 cup diced red onion, 1/4 cup cilantro, 1/4 cup lime juice and 1/2 teaspoon chili powder. Refrigerate for at least 20 minutes. Serve in small bowls with tortilla chips. Prep Time: 25 minutes.

4. Shrimp Scampi: Heat 1 tablespoon olive oil in a large skillet over medium heat. Add 2 minced garlic cloves and cook for 1 minute. Add 1/2 pound cooked shrimp and cook for 2 minutes. Add 2 tablespoons butter, 1/4 cup white wine, 1/4 teaspoon red pepper flakes, and 2 tablespoons chopped parsley. Cook for an additional 1 minute. Serve over cooked pasta or zucchini noodles. Prep Time: 5 minutes.

5. Mussels Marinara: Heat 1 tablespoon olive oil in a large skillet over medium heat. Add 2 minced garlic cloves and 1/2 teaspoon dried oregano. Cook for 1 minute. Add 1/2 pound mussels and 1/2 cup marinara sauce. Cook for 3 minutes, or until the mussels are cooked through. Serve over cooked pasta. Prep Time: 5 minutes.

6. Grilled Fish Tacos: Preheat the oven to 375 degrees F. Place 1/2 pound fish fillet onto a baking sheet lined with parchment paper. Drizzle with olive oil and season with salt, pepper and cumin. Bake for 10 minutes, or until cooked through. Shred the fish and fill warm corn tortillas with the fish, shredded lettuce, diced tomatoes and a dollop of sour cream. Prep Time: 10 minutes.

7. Tuna Salad: In a medium bowl, mix together 1 (5-ounce) can tuna, 1 tablespoon mayonnaise, 1 minced garlic clove, 1/4 teaspoon dried oregano, 1/4 teaspoon dried dill and 1/4 cup diced red onion. Serve in lettuce wraps or on a bed of greens. Prep Time: 5 minutes.

8. Shrimp and Avocado Salad: In a medium bowl, mix together 1/2 pound cooked shrimp, 1 diced avocado, 1/4 cup diced red onion, 1/4 cup diced cucumber and 1/4 cup fresh cilantro. Drizzle with olive oil and the juice of 1 lime. Serve in lettuce wraps or over greens. Prep Time: 5 minutes.

9. Grilled Shrimp Skewers: Preheat the oven to 375 degrees F. Thread 1/2 pound shrimp onto

skewers and place onto a baking sheet lined with parchment paper. Drizzle with olive oil and season with salt, pepper and garlic powder. Bake for 10 minutes, or until cooked through. Serve with a side of tzatziki sauce. Prep Time: 10 minutes.

10. Shrimp Paella: Heat 1 tablespoon olive oil in a large skillet over medium heat. Add 1/2 cup diced onion, 1/2 cup diced red pepper, 1/2 cup diced tomatoes and 2 minced garlic cloves. Cook for 3 minutes. Add 1 cup cooked rice, 1/2 pound cooked shrimp and 1/4 cup frozen peas and cook for an additional 2 minutes. Serve with a side of lemon wedges. Prep Time: 10 minutes.

Ben Georg

Meat beverage:

1. Grilled Lemon-Garlic Chicken: Marinate boneless chicken breasts with olive oil, garlic, lemon juice and oregano for 1 hour. Grill chicken for 5-6 minutes on each side. Serve with a side of quinoa and steamed vegetables. Prep Time: 15 minutes.

2. Baked Fish with Tomatoes and Olives: Preheat oven to 350°F. Place a fillet of white fish on a baking sheet lined with parchment paper. Top with tomatoes, olives, garlic, and herbs. Bake for 15 minutes until cooked through. Serve with a side of roasted potatoes and roasted vegetables. Prep Time: 10 minutes.

3. Mediterranean Stuffed Peppers: Preheat oven to 350°F. Cut bell peppers in half, remove the seeds and place on a baking sheet. In a bowl, mix cooked quinoa, diced tomatoes, spinach, feta cheese, and herbs. Stuff peppers with mixture and bake in preheated oven for 20 minutes. Prep Time: 15 minutes.

4. Mediterranean Turkey Burgers: Mix ground turkey with garlic, diced tomatoes, feta cheese, herbs and spices. Form into patties and cook on a grill or stovetop for 6-7 minutes on each side. Serve with a side of quinoa and steamed vegetables. Prep Time: 10 minutes.

5. Mediterranean Salmon: Preheat oven to 350°F. Place a fillet of salmon on a baking sheet lined with parchment paper. Top with

tomatoes, olives, garlic, and herbs. Bake for 15 minutes until cooked through. Serve with a side of roasted potatoes and roasted vegetables. Prep Time: 10 minutes.

6. Grilled Lamb Skewers: Marinate cubed lamb with olive oil, garlic, lemon juice and oregano for 1 hour. Thread onto skewers and grill for 6-7 minutes on each side. Serve with a side of quinoa and steamed vegetables. Prep Time: 15 minutes.

7. Grilled Vegetable Platter: Preheat grill to medium-high. Slice bell peppers, zucchini, eggplant, and onions into thin slices. Place vegetables on the grill and cook for 6-7 minutes on each side. Serve with a side of quinoa and roasted tomatoes. Prep Time: 10 minutes.

8. Mediterranean Lentil Soup: In a large pot, heat olive oil. Add garlic, onion, celery, carrots and sauté for 5 minutes. Add lentils, diced tomatoes, broth, herbs, and spices. Simmer for 30 minutes. Serve with a side of quinoa and roasted vegetables. Prep Time: 10 minutes.

9. Eggplant Parmesan: Preheat oven to 350°F. Slice eggplant into thin slices and lay on a baking sheet lined with parchment paper. Top with tomatoes, olives, garlic, and herbs. Bake for 15 minutes until cooked through. Serve with a side of roasted potatoes and roasted vegetables. Prep Time: 10 minutes.

10. Grilled Shrimp Skewers: Marinate shrimp with olive oil, garlic, lemon juice and oregano

for 1 hour. Thread onto skewers and grill for 6-7 minutes on each side. Serve with a side of quinoa and steamed vegetables. Prep Time: 15 minutes.

Conclusion

Overall, the Gluten-Free Mediterranean Diet Cookbook is an excellent resource for anyone looking to explore this healthful and delicious diet. With a wide variety of recipes, from simple breakfasts to complex dinner entrees, this book is sure to satisfy all tastes. The book also provides helpful tips and advice for making the transition to a gluten-free lifestyle easier and more enjoyable. With the help of this cookbook, you can enjoy the health benefits of a gluten-free Mediterranean diet without sacrificing flavor or variety.

In conclusion the Gluten-Free Mediterranean Diet Cookbook is an invaluable resource that provides a wealth of knowledge and delicious recipes that are sure to please. Whether you're looking to explore this diet for health reasons or just want to add some delicious and nutritious meals to your repertoire, this cookbook is sure to be a valuable addition to your kitchen.